Hope... and the Hedgehog

Life? Death? And then what?

Our personal quest...

Tom Vaughan

ILLUSTRATED BY MIRANDA HARRIS

THE CHOIR PRESS

ISBN 978-1-78963-290-3

First published in the United Kingdom in 2022 by
The Choir Press, Gloucester

Designed and typeset by David Onyett

DEDICATION

I would like to dedicate this small book to all those who may be questioning faith and searching for answers.

July 2022

With best wishes,

Acknowledgements

In a general way, in the writing of this book, I would like to acknowledge my indebtedness and gratitude to a wide variety of other writers and authors, both alive and long dead, whose work I have been lucky enough to come across and which has inspired and encouraged me.

Amongst the very much alive I must single out Bear Grylls whose seminal book *Soul Fuel* – brilliant in its bite-sized passages of wisdom – has been a constant, daily source of inspiration to me. It is a book that I would unhesitatingly recommend to everyone, particularly as it is a book focused predominantly on faith rather than religion. Also the Rev Elizabeth Cathie for her cerebral and informative weekly Reflections – often scientifically based.

I owe a debt of thanks to those kind enough to have acted as test readers of the manuscript during its various stages of development, and for their valuable feedback and input. Although not exclusively, chief among these were: Georgianna Hewlett, Oliver Vaughan, Claire Dickinson, Nick and Fiona Irens, Paula Snow, David Payne, Harriet Bridgeman and, last but not least, John Handby, one of my atheist friends who enjoyed the irony of my asking him to play devil's advocate in reading the manuscript and who was kind enough to give me a detailed, scholarly critique.

I owe a special debt of thanks to my long-suffering and patient editor, Clive Dickinson, for his skilfulness in knocking the manuscript into shape, and for his encouragement and guidance throughout the project.

I also owe my particular thanks to Miranda Harris (mirandaharris.co.uk) for her considerable artistic talent in creating the charming illustrations that have so brilliantly captured the essence of the book and have added so much to it.

Preface

Hope ... and the Hedgehog was written substantially before the rude arrival of the coronavirus (COVID-19); however, in a spirit of optimism, the brief reference I pay to it is in the past tense as we emerge from the pandemic.

My hope is that readers of this small book will find it readily accessible, thought provoking and, above all, reassuring.

TO BEGIN AT THE BEGINNING

Work on this book began a long time ago (a very long time, if truth be told) before the devastating coronavirus pandemic of 2020. But the arrival of Covid-19 meant the world entered a period of great turmoil, uncertainty and fear on a scale unknown in recent times.

Understandably, the enforced changes in social interaction to combat the virus at the time produced a period of reflection and introspection that played into the subject of this book, with the stark realisation that we cannot always control our own destiny. This book was not conceived with the coronavirus pandemic in mind, but Covid-19 proved to be an unexpected midwife in its delivery.

It also reinforced two of the central themes of the book: that the strongest unifying force we have as humans is love, and that love is not centred on what we can get but on what we can give.

During that time of great anxiety, people found themselves questioning the way they had lived before the imposition of self-isolation, social distancing and lockdown. Similarly, the grim daily reality of the mounting mortality figures all over the world made many people contemplate one of the great taboos of present-day life: the inevitability of their own death. And this, by extension, drew a lot of people to a fundamental questioning of why they are here in the first place.

Few of us can do great things in life, but we can all do small things with great love.

Mother Teresa of Calcutta (20th-century Albanian missionary nun)

I have no recognised qualifications to write this book. I have had no scientific, philosophical or theological training of any kind; my performance at school was hardly spectacular.

In the light of this admission, there will be those who question how I have the audacity to try to write a book that deals with subjects as profound as life, death and then what? My answer is one of the more important life lessons I did get from my rather sketchy school days. We were regularly told, 'Always remember that no one has the right to limit your ambitions.'

No one has the right, either, to prevent any of us from asking questions or seeking help in finding answers to them. That is why throughout this book I have enlisted the assistance of a wide selection of people with an equally wide range of experience and understanding of the topics I wanted to explore. Their thoughts and ideas are interwoven with my own to produce what I hope will be an accessible and reassuring account of one person's attempt to make sense of it all. Importantly, as I trust what follows shows, the key word is 'hope'; for, even in our darkest hours, hope is our guiding light.

Hope lifts us out of the rubble of our failures, our pain and our fear to rise above what at one point seemed insurmountable. Our ability to endure, to persevere, to overcome is fuelled by this one, seemingly innocuous, ingredient called hope.

Erwin McManus (author and filmmaker)

And the hedgehog?

Let me explain.

*   *   *

I chose to call this book *Hope ... and the Hedgehog* because hope is one of the principal drivers we resort to as human beings when confronted with a challenge to which there is no obvious solution. In the case of this book, that challenge is a very prickly issue: how we came into existence. It is an issue that we are all drawn to, but at the same time we do not want to handle or investigate too closely. Like the proverbial elephant in the room, we know that little hedgehog is there, we just prefer to leave it be – even if, in the end, there is no avoiding it. With the right attitude and mindset however, it need not be disturbing. It can instead become like the piece of grit in the oyster that makes the pearl.

This is not to deny the genuine doubt that many people experience when faced with choices and decisions as momentous as the ones raised here, because we all live with doubt and even the staunchest believer can experience doubt at times.

In God we doubt ... better honest doubt than dishonest faith.

John Humphrys (veteran British reporter and former titan of the BBC *Today* programme)

So, let me start with the questions I asked myself.

Do you know where you came from? Do you know why you are here, or where you are going? Do you know what the plan is for your life – or even if there is any plan? There are those of course who hold that we have no purpose – or need of one.

...and all the while that little hedgehog is observing and wondering

I should make it clear at the outset that this book does not promote religion – any religion. Although, in some cases, religion can provide a path to belief, it is better to question and be open to the concept of a creative force first, before becoming influenced by any specific doctrinal teaching or guidance.

At the same time, we cannot ignore that religion of every creed is so imbedded in human society that it forms an integral part of our lives. To mention a few examples: much of the world still counts days from before (BC) and after (AD) the birth of Christ; most of the world uses the Gregorian calendar, with seven-day weeks ending on a Sunday; Christmas and Easter are major events in the Christian calendar, as are Hanukkah, Shabbat and Rosh Hashanah in the Jewish calendar, Ramadan and Eid al-Fitr in the Islamic calendar, Diwali in the Hindu calendar, Gurupurbs in the Sikh calendar, or Paryushana in the Jain calendar. Some of these, including Christmas, are of course based on earlier 'pagan' festivals, such as the Winter Solstice.

While not ignoring religion, this book sets out to sidestep it: to explore the possibility faith offers without religion getting in the way. This is faith as a principle, if you like, as opposed to faith as a precept laid down as part of any religious observance. This is the faith that provides hope in the eternal quest to find the meaning of life – an answer for which humankind has always been searching, if often in secret! However faintly, it is the human condition to have the impulse of faith. Little faith is better than no faith because at least it holds out hope.

We live in an age of science and reason, where those who hold to a secular view of the world are scornful of faith because being unable either to see it or measure it as a reality, they are unable to believe it.

And yet, so much of our scientific understanding is itself taken on faith – not of course religious faith – but nevertheless on faith that one thing will lead to another: that the sun will rise every morning, that the moon will follow its own idiosyncratic passage across the heavens, even that a light will illuminate when we turn on a switch.

By definition, faith is a belief in something without yet having sufficient evidence to be completely certain of its truth.

Human beings must be known to be loved; but divine beings must be loved to be known.

Blaise Pascal (17th-century French philosopher, mathematician and physicist)

One of the only things we can be certain of in life is change, therefore we should embrace change when it happens, learn from it and, if possible, find contentment in accepting it. With this in mind, I broke my quest into three parts: the plot, the question, the dilemma.

In the simplest of terms, the plot is this: we are born, we live, and we die. None of us know how long the middle part of the plot will be – but, although we would rather not think about it, we know for certain what the end is. Even planet earth will not continue forever; our world is finite, as are we.

The question is: why are we born, why are we here, is there any purpose to life beyond what we accomplish on earth – and, if there is, what is it? Perhaps even, why is human life so seemingly random in its fairness? These questions apply to all of us whether we have any religious belief, or none. Most of us take the many extraordinary wonders of this world for granted, and we quite happily take so much of daily life on faith, is it not paradoxical that we seem unwilling to extend this to our very existence?

This book does not attempt to present any definitive argument so much as to make the proposition that, between only two possible explanations for the existence of life, there is a greater likelihood of the one over the other. In doing so, there has to be an acceptance that it is based on current knowledge and thinking: scientific, philosophical, theological and even circumstantial. Thus, allowance needs to be made for the possibility of change as our knowledge base evolves and increases.

The simple things are also the most extraordinary things and only the wise can see them.

Paulo Coelho (Brazilian author)

Attempting to explore (rather than answer) these questions, leads to the dilemma, in which, by a process of thought, and the elimination of alternative possibilities, we are eventually forced to face the fact that there can be only two answers. Our origin and existence are either the result of a huge cosmic accident, a rather dark joke; or life has meaning, albeit one we cannot yet understand or be privy to.

Arguably, our decision over which it is becomes the most important one we will ever make because it will influence the rest of our lives. If we decide that life does have a meaning, a purpose and a destiny – then it leaves open the possibility of there being some sort of creator, or God by another name.

Hold fast to dreams. For if dreams die, life is a broken-winged bird that cannot fly.

Langston Hughes (American poet, playwright and social activist)

As I have said, this book avoids getting bogged down in the dogma of religious teachings or beliefs; that is not its purpose. Unfortunately, the trappings, rules, fundamentalist outlooks, mystiques and ceremonies of many religions can often be a smokescreen obscuring a simple questing belief in a divine creator, or a higher being.

So, this book attempts to focus on what we call life, for however long or short it is. It sets out to explore the optimistic probability of something, rather than the pessimistic certainty of nothing. It is not intended as any kind of strident wake-up call – more a gentle nudge to thinking about something important because, ultimately, it affects us all.

But, take note of what the German existential philosopher Paul Tillich has to say on the subject, 'Whoever reflects earnestly on the meaning of life is on the verge of an act of faith.'

For those who have chosen to put their faith in some sort of intelligent design, there remains the challenge of trying to imagine, even dimly, the magnitude of what was involved in the staggeringly complex process of creation. Faith is lived through a struggle with darkness and confusion.

This book does not set out to preach or convert; but, having evaluated the idea of life as a random fluke of cosmic activity, it seeks to explore what it considers to be the greater likelihood of the alternative.

It is only with the heart that one can see rightly that, what is essential, is invisible to the human eye.

Antoine de Saint-Exupéry (French airman, writer and poet, author of *The Little Prince*)

DEATH WHERE IS THY STING?

Though it be in the power of the weakest arm to take away life, it is not in the strongest to deprive us of death.

Sir Thomas Browne (17th-century English polymath, physician and esoteric observer of life)

Despite these wise words from 400 years ago, kings, queens, emperors, pharaohs and paranoid individuals have always sought ways to cheat death.

The first Emperor of China, Qin Shi Huang, founder of the Qin Dynasty who reigned from 247 to 220BC, having declared himself 'Emperor God' spent much of his time searching the world for the elusive herb that would enable him to live forever. His equally doomed back-up plan was to enter the next world, entombed with all his wealth, protected by an army of 6,000 terracotta soldiers.

Important Egyptians, Greeks, Romans, Saxons, Normans and many others adopted the same futile methods, sometimes even choosing to be buried with chariots amongst other trappings of status and wealth. However misguided, such practices unarguably demonstrate a belief in – or hope for – something after death.

In more recent times a number of eccentric millionaires and billionaires have taken up the quest to preserve their lives through increasingly bizarre methods. These include having their bodies (in some cases, just heads and brains!) deep-frozen to be thawed out and 'revived' at some unspecified time in the future, when they believe that science will have found the answer to immortality.

Founded in 1972, a company called Alcor, based in the deserts of Arizona, caters to those who wish to have their remains placed in a cryogenic deep freeze to await 'reanimation'. At current rates, freezing your head costs $80,000 and your entire body $200,000.

Others, thinking about their own refuge and survival within a shorter time frame, prepare for an imagined Armageddon by building bunkers, ranging from the relatively modest to whole, heavily-fortified, compounds to which they think they can retreat and be safe.

Invariably, such people have lost sight of the fact that at some point they are going to die anyway. They do not consider how depressing and disappointing it might be to survive the end of civilisation as we know it. Such a colossal and devastating calamity would result in: no, or very limited human contact; no law and order; no infra-structure; no doctors; no medicines; no supermarkets; shops; restaurants; food supply; phone service; electricity; plumbing; television – the list of deprivation goes on and on. As with any game, the game of life, played without rules or order, would be no fun and would quickly turn into chaos, leading to anger and violence.

There is nothing new in this fixation with survival at all costs. More than 3,000 years ago, in what is now Turkey but was then known as Cappadocia, the Hittites excavated subterranean caves in the sides of mountains to act as shelters against any end-of-the-world scenario. The ancient Egyptians were obsessed with mummification as a process of preservation for an afterlife; in some respects we are no different in our futile attempts to live forever.

It is interesting that this fear of death and the fevered desire to cling on to life seem to be particularly prevalent amongst the rich, despite the fact that we enter this world with absolutely nothing and leave it with absolutely nothing! One of the latest fads for those in search of eternal youth and immortality is to have their 'old' blood reinvigorated with injections of new, fresh, young blood.

The latest high profile figures to have joined this search for immortality – or at least breath-taking life extensions – reputedly include Jeff Bezos of Amazon, Larry Page, co-founder of Google, Peter Thiel and Yuri Milner.

They are just a few of the more prominent Silicon Valley tech entrepreneurs or investors, making eye-watering investments in what are essentially mostly start-up enterprises, the principal mission of which is to find the holy grail of immortality – or at least healthy life extension. Although perhaps taking different approaches, companies such as Altos, Calico and Unity Biotech are all involved in this research.

No man is rich enough to buy back his past.

Oscar Wilde

However, it seems all these attempts are likely to prove futile, as revealed in a 2017 study by Professor Joanna Masel from the University of Arizona. Her research, published in the *Proceedings of the National Academy of Sciences*, uses a mathematical model to demonstrate the inevitability of death regardless of whichever attempt at immortality is resorted to.

The undeniable fact is that absolutely everything in this world is decaying or degrading all the time, whether it is human, animal, vegetable, mineral or material. The only difference is the varying speeds with which this inevitability is occurring.

Planet earth itself is not exempt from this inexorable process! Thus, natural life cannot become an end in itself because it bears within it the seed of death.

The hard truth is we are all born to die, but it is perhaps in dying that we become part of the cycle of life.

It doesn't matter how rich, successful, famous or important we may become, we can never be entirely insulated from periods of introspection about where we came from and where we might be going.

Like it or not, in line with the Chinese proverb that says, 'A person who asks a question may look foolish for five minutes, but one who does not ask a question remains foolish forever', we are faced with some key questions about our existence.

'What, if anything, is the purpose of life?'

'What, if anything, happens after I die?'

'Is death the end, or is there something more?'

Dealing with the last of these head-on, how much better would it be to see death not as a dreaded spectre at the end of our life, but rather more as a friend paving the way for a continuation of a fascinating journey?

Most of the trouble in the world is caused by people wanting to be important.

T S Elliot (poet, critic and dramatist)

A hundred thousand years hence, no one, however great they may seem now, will be remembered from this era. We are just drops of water in the ocean of time in the infinite expanse of the cosmos. Human greatness is a temporary illusion, a passing irrelevance. What will remain of our legacy is the building of humility, service and love laid down as an example to those who follow us.

> **If you attempt to talk to a dying man about sports or business, he is no longer interested.**
> **He now sees other things as more important.**
> **People who are dying recognise what we often forget, that we are standing on the brink of another world.**
>
> William Law (17/18th-century English priest and mystic)

Millennia of history have shown us that death remains the natural conclusion to life. Yet, unfortunately, many people live their whole lives in fear of death, so much so that, in insidiously and darkly subtle ways, it robs them of the full joy of living. What matters is not to lose the joy of living in the fear of dying. Corrie ten Boom, the Dutch Second World War resistance hero and writer, put it well when she observed, 'Worry does not empty tomorrow of its sorrow; it empties today of its strength.'

So, making friends with what is our unavoidable destiny is the way to a calm acceptance of the inevitable – as well as freeing us from the fear of death itself. For the one thing we can be sure of is that no one gets out alive!

As someone with a wry sense of humour facing an early death said in recent times, 'However you look at it we are all of us on the same journey, with the same inevitable outcome, on a flight departure to which only some are selected for Priority Boarding'.

In that same vein there is light-hearted wisdom in the

words of *New York Times* bestselling author Anne Lamott who said, 'I view death as mostly a significant change of address'.

Courage is not the absence of fear, because to be brave we must first be afraid before we can conquer that fear. Paradoxically, the moment closest to death, when life is stripped back to the essentials of survival, is often when a person feels most alive. This happened to one passenger on the famous US Airways Flight 1549 that crash-landed in New York's Hudson River in 2009. After being asked how it had felt to have survived this, he famously responded, 'I was alive before the crash, but now I'm really alive'.

The celebrated Russian novelist Fyodor Dostoyevsky had a life-changing moment when, after being sentenced to death, he was blindfolded and led to stand in front of a firing squad. Just as rifles were raised and he heard triggers being cocked, word came that the czar had granted him a last-minute reprieve. His sentence was commuted to eight years in a harsh Siberian prison.

While there, incarcerated with hardened criminals, he was enormously impressed by their faith. But it was his experience in front of the firing squad that led him to believe that life was a gift and the experience gave him a heightened appreciation for every day thereafter.

Because human nature seeks recognition, exaltation and adulation, we often withhold our gratitude in failing to recognise that everything we have is in fact a gift: our intelligence, our talents, our wealth. (There is a theory that the word 'present' may have derived from the concept that every day was valued as a gift from God.)

We need to understand, and constantly remind ourselves, just how short life is. It is a daily practice for some Buddhists to keep in mind that 'Death is certain, only the time of death is uncertain'. This is not done morbidly, but in the knowledge that it enriches each day with a heightened sense of being fully alive. It is the very fragility of life that makes it so precious.

... overwhelming relief at the unexpected chance to live again

Man, because he sacrifices his health in order to make money, then has to sacrifice his money to recover his health. Then he is so anxious about the future that he does not enjoy the present. The result being that he does not live in the present or the future; instead he lives as if he is never going to die, and then dies having never really lived.

The Dalai Lama

Perspectives change as we get older, and most of us realise and understand how ephemeral and unimportant possessions and the trappings of our lives are in the overall scheme of things. If we are lucky, this allows us to see and focus on how much more important people, family, friendships and love really are.

It can also be instructive to look at ancient history to get a better perspective of the transitory nature of life. Archaeology and what written and visual evidence there is confirm the existence and scale of ancient civilisations. But, comparatively speaking, so little detail survives that, beyond its intrinsic historical interest, it is of little relevance to our lives today.

Whether we like it or not, we all must confront the fact of our own mortality. Interlinked with this are the joint questions of how we came into being, where we might have come from, and where we might be going?

Each of us has a personal responsibility to face these questions. Although, in the Western world at least, we seem to have become almost genetically programmed not to think about the end of the 'plot' too much, until, through age, illness or other circumstances we may be forced to do so. However unrealistic it is, we tend to carry on, often making far-reaching decisions as if the merry-go-round of life will never stop.

This way of thinking – or not thinking – is not limited to our own mortality. It is often applied to other 'unpleasant' subjects we would rather not grapple with, such as: pensions, politics, a visit to the dentist, or even the diagnosis of a serious illness.

There is an analogy here with our tendency to avoid delayed gratification in favour of instant gratification. Experiments have shown that if you offer someone a choice of £100 now or £101 in twelve months, they will always choose £100 now. If you were to make the delay worthwhile by offering, say, £120 or £150, then you will get takers. Perhaps it is the entirely unknown 'reward', from an unknowable future, that discourages people from contemplating what, if anything, happens to us after death?

It might be worth noting here that Steve Jobs, the founder of Apple, who was well known for his enquiring mind and his fascination with the genius of innovative design, left a tantalising reaction to the moment of his death. According to his sister, just prior to death, he looked off into the middle distance with an expression that suggested he could see something. The last three words he spoke were: 'wow ... wow ... WOW!' This of course poses the question of what he might have 'seen' during the transition from life to death. It is made all the more interesting coming from a man disciplined with the rational 'scientific' mind of a technological engineer.

Aleksandr Solzhenitsyn, world-famous Nobel Laureate and outspoken Russian dissident, was raised as a Christian but lost his faith while he was still a young man and became a firm believer in both atheism and Marxism/Leninism. However, as a result of his experiences in prison and the harshness of the camps where he was incarcerated, he became a philosophically minded Eastern Orthodox Christian in later life.

In May 1983, Solzhenitsyn received The Templeton Prize, an annual award granted to a living person who, in the estimation of the judges, 'has made an exceptional contribution to affirming life's spiritual dimension, whether through insight, discovery, or practical works'.

The title of the address Solzhenitsyn gave on receiving it encapsulated for me his spiritual and intellectual journey to that point. Viewing the dystopian nadir of his experiences, he headed his renowned address with the words: 'Godlessness: The First Step to the Gulag'.

We must accept finite disappointment but never lose infinite hope.

Dr Martin Luther King Jnr

I once asked the owner of a world-famous shipyard that specialises in building superyachts for the very rich if there was any kind of pattern to indicate how many yachts his clients were usually good for. His reply was intriguing. 'Two and a half' was his succinct answer.

The first is their dream yacht, until they sail it to some of the world's most exotic and glamorous marinas, where their peer group like to congregate and play.

After a bit, the proximity of many even larger and more beautiful yachts than theirs begins to rankle and sow the seeds of discontent. Eventually this reaches such a pitch that they come back and ask the shipyard to build them another yacht, substantially larger than the first.

So, the process begins again and before too long they are back to order the third and final yacht. But, given the time it takes to design, build and equip these huge boats, they rarely live long enough to take delivery of the third one!

It was G K Chesterton who once quipped, 'To be clever enough to get money, one must be stupid enough to want it.' Although a little unfair if taken literally, its succinct resonance carries a warning!

Another, rather poignant, example of the self-deceiving nature of human vanity is that of Julius Drewe, the founder of the highly successful Home and Colonial Stores. Having made his fortune, he decided to establish a dynasty, and in so doing leave a lasting family legacy, by building himself a proper castle (the last ever to be constructed in the UK).

Castle Drogo in Devon is not a 'cardboard' castle, but the real thing. Work started on Julius' fifty-fifth birthday in 1911. Tragically, in 1917 his eldest son, Adrian, was killed in the First World War. Simultaneously, wartime austerity and increased taxation imposed a big financial burden.

The combination of these events appears to have robbed poor Julius of all purpose and joy in living. Even when reduced to roughly a third of its original Lutyens' design, Castle Drogo was still not completed until 1930. Although Julius Drewe was able to live in it during the last five years of construction, he died barely twelve months after its completion. His peaceful occupancy of this lifelong dream lasted just a year.

Now a National Trust property, it stands as an example of the ephemeral nature of material things in terms of human ambition, however grand they may be in worldly terms. Although there is no way of knowing if it applied to Julius Drewe or not, those who ambitiously seek such worldly prizes are often ready to sacrifice anything for them: their time, their energies, their wealth, without sparing so much as a thought for the idea that their eternal destination might, at the very least, be worthy of equal time and energy.

Life is but a bridge, walk confidently across but build no house upon it.

Indian proverb

Another example of this type of *folie de grandeur* dates back to 1828 when, infuriated at having failed to buy the magnificent ruins of Goodrich Castle in Herefordshire, Sir William Rush Meyrick – who made his immense fortune out of procurement for the armed services – bought the next promontory up the River Wye and set about building an even bigger castle. This he called Goodrich Court.

As happened to Julius Drewe, Sir William's son predeceased him and he himself died in 1848 after living in Goodrich Court for only twenty years. Today, the substantial ruins of Goodrich Castle, which date from Norman times, stand firm, strong and much visited, whereas not a single stone of Goodrich Court remains – its very existence barely remembered. Similar examples abound around the world; it is a very human temptation.

If you own something you cannot part with, then you don't own it; it owns you.

Albert Schweitzer (Alsatian Physician, Philosopher and Writer)

Modern society reflects a growing tendency to confuse worldly status with our true significance as individuals. If we are rich, have a big house (or even houses), with the right car, an enviable or glittering career, the perfect family, a film-star body, we can relish having our success validated by the envy of others.

Unfortunately, this is very short-term thinking. Real success and long-term happiness are more easily found in being selfless rather than selfish. Material acquisitiveness is almost always impossible to satisfy because, however much you get, it is never enough. In fact, the harder we chase material possessions the less they satisfy us.

I have made many millions, but they have brought me no happiness.

John D Rockefeller

Sadly, many successful people – most not nearly as rich as Rockefeller – often approach the end of life wondering what it was all about, and whether the pressure to be a financial success was worth the sacrifice of personal happiness. Paraphrasing words from Bear Grylls: we need to guard against falling into the common trap of loving money and using people, instead of using money and loving people.

In our desire for recognition and affirmation we lose sight of the fact that what we are really seeking is to love and be loved. The nineteenth-century French novelist and dramatist Victor Hugo put it well when he noted, 'The greatest happiness in life is the conviction that we are loved, loved for ourselves, or rather loved in spite of ourselves.'

If you judge people, you have no time to love them.

Mother Teresa of Calcutta

All of this is made easier by the fact that, to some extent, humans do live in the moment. We often find, for example, that even a photograph from a holiday of a lifetime, or some other highlight in our lives, does not enable us to recapture fully the intense magic of the actual moment, which, although not extinguished, is now a diminishing memory.

There is another side to this, of course. Just as precious memories begin to fade, so do painful ones: the sadness of selling a cherished family home, or the agony of losing a person we love – excruciating as that may be at the time. In due course, some of us find it harder and harder even to recall the faces of those we have known and loved.

A slightly more scientific analogy for the possibility of life after death – or some form of resurrection – might be to consider that, if a blob of mercury can be shattered and then, by application of a different process, completely reunited and reformed into its original mass, indistinguishable from the first, why should this not be possible for humans under the influence, or in the plan or will, of an intelligent designer – or, Prime Mover for those more inclined towards the AI/virtual world.

We live and move through time, while our hearts, our destiny – quietly but insistently – point towards something else, beyond time into eternity.

Anonymous

It was the great English economist, John Maynard Keynes, who famously said, 'We must give a lot of thought to the future. It is where we are going to live for the rest of our lives'. Had he not been an ardent agnostic he might have added the words: '. . . and beyond'.

At some time or another there is a quest in almost every human being to find meaning in their lives; and this is a hole that cannot be filled through the acquisition of power, or great wealth. Some are able to find meaning in the here and now through the pursuit of worthwhile achievement. But, rich or poor, we all carry the same chronic illness. It is called death: inevitable and unavoidable. The strange and, unfortunately, sometimes painful process of dying may make us understandably apprehensive (even downright terrified!), but when our grip on life grows inexorably ever fainter, death itself need not be either frightening or depressing.

Consider the clumsy, slow-moving, earthbound caterpillar that in defiance of imagination will eventually be transformed into a beautiful butterfly, able to fly and dance lightly on the breeze. It remains the same creature just in a different form. Or a tiny seed that contains and protects hidden life for many years (some seeds from pre-biblical times have been successfully germinated). The dry, brown, shrivelled outer casing gives no hint of the life contained therein. However, once planted and tended, when the new shoot emerges from the soil, no trace of the former wizened seed state remains; what has risen from it is vibrant and visibly changed.

Logic can only take you from A to B. Imagination can take you everywhere.

Albert Einstein (20th-century physicist and
founder of the theory of relativity)

I would like to use two other quite simple examples that readers may find helpful. The first concerns what might happen after death, while also offering a possible explanation of why the quality of human life on earth might be perceived as being so unfairly distributed.

... happy metamorphosis

Imagine you are looking at the back of any tapestry, perhaps a contemporary Archie Brennan work, or what, despite its images of violence, many consider to be the world's most beautiful example, the famous Bayeux Tapestry in France. All you can see on the reverse side is a discordant jumble of messy threads that form no picture and make no discernible sense. A metaphor for the messiness of life? Perhaps. But what if, after death, we are able to look at the front of this great piece of art and through its exquisite workmanship finally come to understand and appreciate the sheer beauty of its perfection – could this not be a metaphor for an afterlife, or heaven?

For the second example, imagine twins in their mother's womb shortly before birth. As the process of birth begins, one twin says to the other, 'We are warm, well fed and content. I don't want to leave this safe place and be born. We have no idea what is out there!'

This twin resists birth with all his or her might. The other twin, recognising the inevitability of birth, embraces it and is the first to be born into a new life, one so much better than in the womb! Might this be a metaphor for our attitude towards death?

If I live on as love in the hearts of those I've left behind, I have not died.

Mark Twain (19th-century American writer and humorist)

Those who have seen a corpse – especially straight after the moment of death – often remark that a dead body, although peaceful, so quickly looks as if it has been lifeless forever, as if that person had never been alive. This is often the moment when agnostics are at least tempted to believe in a higher rhythm or order in life.

Is the factor that sets apart the living from the dead what some people would call the spirit, and others the soul? If it is, it raises the question of where did the spirit or soul go after leaving the body? To nothingness, or to something more? A soul travelling in eternal time?

There are, of course, many who claim to have had some after-death experience, but the one I find most compelling is that of Jonathan Bryan. Bryan was born with cerebral palsy and his parents were told he would never communicate. However, these wonderful people refused to give up on their son and, despite his being 'locked in' with overwhelming physical limitations (he is unable to speak or do anything for himself), they have been rewarded with the knowledge that Jonathan is in there, astute and alive.

Jonathan's condition renders him vulnerable to infection. When he was eleven a particularly aggressive respiratory virus almost claimed his life. Close to death, he describes a vivid, dreamlike, vision of himself in which he could speak and play in Jesus' Garden, after being told that that is where he was.

Able-bodied, free to run and do as he wished, Jonathan badly wanted to stay there. But he did not. He returned to his worldly existence even though, as he says, 'it was the toughest decision of my life to come back.'

Now, aided by a computer, Jonathan has learned to communicate with eye movements. Intelligent and articulate, he completed his autobiography *Eye Can Write* in which he recorded this telling experience among other similarly moving accounts.

Presented with this 'insight' from someone speaking with the innocence of childhood, who are we to dismiss Jonathan's experience as purely hallucinatory; or for that matter to discount the possibility of parallel universes that it raises? We have countless evidence of imprints from the past, but no evidence of imprints of the future – only indications.

Somewhere between good and evil there is a garden, bye and bye I shall meet you there.

Rumi (13th-century Persian mystical poet
and Islamic scholar)

AN EVEN BRIEFER HISTORY OF TIME

So, what was the very beginning of life? The Big Bang which led to the creation of life as a purely natural phenomenon?

Way back when, billions of years ago in the history of the universe, there was 'something'. There had to be, because even the most sceptical of scientists or the most ardent of atheists must all agree that you cannot create something out of nothing. Therefore, at some point, the spark that ignited life had to have been set in motion or 'created' ... even if, following any so-called Big Bang, this might only have been the most elemental of gases or rudimentary microscopic organisms from a primordial soup.

Think hard on that deliberate choice of the word 'something'! It is only the: what, why, where and how that something – that spark, that force – came into being that is up for discussion here, along with whatever we choose to call it.

The eminent theoretical astrophysicist Professor Stephen Hawking got as far as identifying the beginning of life as 'the occurrence of tiny atomic fluctuations within the atmosphere'. But this still leaves open the question of what preceded these 'fluctuations'?

In his seminal book *A Brief History of Time*, Hawking explained that if scientists were able to develop a set of equations that described every component in the universe, 'it would be the ultimate triumph of human reason ... for then we should know the mind of God'. Although, true to his atheist persuasion, he later explained this statement as having been essentially a metaphor stating, 'you can say the laws of physics are the work of God, but that is more a definition of God than proof of his existence.'

Science is not only compatible with spirituality; it is a profound source of spirituality.

Carl Sagan (American astronomer, cosmologist and astrophysicist)

Although Hawking held no hope for, or belief in, an afterlife (interestingly, making his position on this point similar to that of the Sadducees of biblical times, and some of the Jewish faith today), even that does not necessarily preclude the possibility of a creator, or intelligent designer, of the life we know and have.

Questioning with an open mind all his life, there are some indications of uncertainty even in Stephen Hawking. Towards the very end, this giant of a thinker was a big enough man to turn his back on his signature hypothesis about the first instant of his Big Bang theory, when he had proposed a 'no-boundary' theory – later depicted as a pivotal moment in his 2014 biopic *The Theory of Everything*.

It is intriguing – and tempting – to think that within his questing mind, Stephen Hawking might have been more an enigmatic agnostic than a militant atheist, as was so brilliantly portrayed by Eddie Redmayne in his

Oscar-winning performance. Hawking was certainly not angrily dogmatic in the way of some prominent, so-called 'confident atheists', humanists or even pantheists, who would do well to reflect on Voltaire's wise admonition below.

Doubt is not a pleasant condition, but certainty is an absurd one.

Voltaire (18th-century French writer)

In any discussion or argument between an atheist and a believer (as in a person of faith) there exists a likelihood that the atheist, presupposing the believer to be coming from a religious perspective, will claim that science supports atheism. When, in fact, it is the same science that can, and often does, point towards the faith held by the believer.

Creationism and evolution are not opposing theories or positions, as many seem to suppose. In allowing for the possibility of a guiding hand behind intelligent design, it would be sensible to acknowledge that evolution forms an essential role in creation. In fact, it could be said that the intricacies of evolution go a long way towards endorsing the greater likelihood of intelligent design over a completely random happening.

Respecting this premise, those with a firm faith and those who believe in something more than a cosmic accident but are not sure what, should always be respectful, tolerant and accepting of the opposing views of others, treating them as they would wish their own views to be received and accommodated.

Life, as we know it, is not – and never has been – static. It is constantly evolving and will always continue to do so. Scientists of the atheist persuasion, and those who have faith in something beyond science, all have a shared wonder of nature and the universe. Einstein himself referred to the extraordinary sense of the mysterious as his 'cosmic religious experience.'

Contrary to popular misconception, Einstein was not an atheist so much as an ardent agnostic, who had no

... in the beginning ... the spark?

time whatever for any form of organised religion. He dismissed the Bible as a collection of fairy stories. Nor was he religious in the traditional sense, beyond his conviction that there was probably a guiding 'force' behind the coordinated rhythm of the universe. In one of his more famous remarks on the subject Einstein said, 'God is clever, but not dishonest'. In effect, he leaned much more towards the pantheism espoused by the seventeenth-century Dutch philosopher Baruch Spinoza, which is discussed later.

Education is the progressive realisation of our ignorance.

Albert Einstein

It is worth reflecting on the fact that Einstein is far from alone in his dismissal of the Bible and similar religious texts. Voltaire, the eighteenth-century philosopher, who was probably more atheist than agnostic, predicted that the Bible would be obsolete and have gone out of circulation within a hundred years. It remains the bestselling book of all time.

On his deathbed, a priest asked Voltaire, 'Do you renounce Satan?' True to his agnostic – if not downright atheist – leanings, Voltaire is reputed to have replied: 'This is no time to be losing friends.'

I like to think that the priest might have had enough of a sense of humour to appreciate this riposte!

Carl Sagan, the renowned American astronomer, cosmologist and astrophysicist, posed the rhetorical question, 'Who is more humble? The scientist who looks at the universe with an open mind and accepts whatever the universe has to teach us, or somebody who says everything in this book must be considered the literal truth and never mind the fallibility of all the human beings involved.'

Without meaning to disparage the opinion of others, it is hard not to share this view when so much of the Bible is contradictory. But perhaps that also says something about people's understanding – or misunderstanding – of what the Bible really is. First off, it is not a single book in the accepted meaning of the word 'book' and is better not being read as such. The Bible is more a collection of books, written over different periods of time by different people, and is therefore far better viewed as a compact reference library; but one in which individual texts or extracts should not be co-opted as weapons, or misused to support particular doctrinal positions. (This is equally applicable to the sacred tenets of other religious works like the Torah or the Koran.) Such thinking would be unsafe and unsound.

In the same way, it is patently absurd for Christians to believe that the only way to salvation is through Jesus Christ, since this would exclude all those of different faiths, including followers of Judaism and Islam, both of which share a common root with Christianity in acknowledging descent from Abraham. It would be safer for Christians to accept that the only way for them to find salvation is through Jesus Christ, leaving open alternative paths for non-Christians – as is explicitly implied in the New Testament.

> **Most people are bothered by those passages in scripture which they cannot understand; but as for me, I always noticed that the passages in scripture which trouble me most are those I do understand.**
>
> Mark Twain

Don't Know Much About a Science Book

Despite its rapid progress, science still has its limitations, as even eminent practitioners like Dr Phillip Goff, a philosopher of science at Durham University, readily admits in his observation:

Physical science doesn't really tell us what 'matter' actually is ... it can only tell us what matter does and how it behaves ... physics tells us absolutely nothing about the intrinsic nature of 'matter'. What philosophers of science have realised is that, for all its richness, physics is confined to the behaviour of matter.

Energy and mass are interchangeable: they are different forms of the same thing. So, science reveals to us that everything in existence is both matter and energy at the same time – or some might call it matter and spirit – co-existing as one.

As with so many things in life, all of science is, and has always been, on a continuous learning curve and there remains much more to be discovered. Self-evidently, we do not know what future discoveries will inform and maybe change our current thinking. What we do know is that uncertainty, questioning and testing are the engines of science!

Given the catastrophes and disasters that occur in the natural world, it could be construed that the universe is engaged in some sort of supernatural conflict that forms the background to life on planet Earth. While apparently destructive on the one hand, such momentous events could be viewed as similar to the processes that forge hardened steel alloys, through which the mechanical properties of the material are tempered and improved.

The first gulp from the glass of natural sciences will make you an atheist, but at the bottom of the glass God is waiting for you.

Werner Heisenberg (Nobel Prize-winning father of quantum physics)

Despite his brilliant colossus of a brain, it should be permissible to allow that Stephen Hawking may not always have been right about everything. No one can prove one way or the other whether there is anything more to our existence after we die; atheists, humanists and pantheists do not believe there is. But we can consider the circumstantial evidence of those whose integrity can be trusted, and who have had some direct experience that might provide a clue.

As noted by Sarah Knapton, science editor of *The Times*, 'The world of quantum exists in a baffling fog of uncertainty where particles change states, pop in and out of existence for seemingly no reason and interact at speeds faster than light.'

The American theoretical physicist Richard Feynman once said, 'I think it is safe to say nobody understands quantum mechanics.'

More recently, the highly respected theoretical physicist Carlo Rovelli said, 'We don't understand quantum mechanics yet. If there is something clear it is that it is not clear.' None of which means that quantum is an invalid science, just because we do not yet fully understand it. This is where the interaction, the interconnectedness, of quantum theory involving quantum physics and quantum mechanics, touch on time itself.

Impossible to nail down, time is something as slippery as it is mysterious. Yet we are all fellow travellers through time, which is something we take so completely for granted we seldom, if ever, even think about it. Because we are alive, time exists for us; we bring it to life and give it meaning. The present moment is all. Because each day brings us a small step closer to death, right now – this very moment – is of great importance.

Lulled into a false sense of security by what we perceive as the permanence and stability surrounding us, it becomes easy to deceive ourselves over how ephemeral life is and forget we have no permanent home here on earth. Without knowing when we are going to die, or even for sure what tomorrow will bring, we live within the dimension of time but walk on the brink of eternity ... just as planet Earth revolves in a similarly precarious state.

The Western world thinks of time as a line, with a beginning and an end, whereas in Asian cultural traditions many people think of time as a circle. This represents a rejection of nothingness, replacing a blank hereafter with a sense of a forever. Thus, a countdown to zero may be thought of as death, but not as an ending. This way of thinking holds out the prospect of the infinite, in which what some would call the soul, others the spirit, will survive physical death.

Although tamed and named by humans, time is an astronomical phenomenon that occurs with reliable regularity in giving us the days and nights by which we are able to measure it. The question I put to myself is, 'What, or who, created this perfectly balanced astronomical measurement, without which life as we know it could not exist?'

Time is part of eternity, therefore time wasted is lost for all eternity.

Anonymous

TO INFINITY AND BEYOND

In 2019 NASA astronaut, engineer and artist Nicole Stott spent 104 days on the International Space Station and, although already a person of faith, she said afterwards that the experience only served to strengthen that belief. In her own words:

> ... to look at the Earth from space ... nothing prepares you for it. It is more stunning ... just like overwhelmingly, impressively beautiful. The Earth glows. It is crystal clear and iridescent and translucent ... like the brightest light bulb you can imagine, with all those colours we know to be Earth splattered on it. And it is set against the blackest black I've ever seen. It looks like it is alive ... like its own living, breathing organism and you realise that everyone you know, everyone you don't know, is down there on that planet, giving a tremendous sense of interconnectivity.

Could this have been, for her, a privileged glimpse of creation? The iridescent glow of planet Earth to which she refers is the result of the global photosynthesis taking place as the fundamental process of life, a process unique to our 'home'.

On Valentine's Day (14 February) 1990, the *Voyager I* spacecraft took pictures of Earth around four million miles (approximately six million kilometres) away. These showed Earth as an infinitesimal pinpoint of light, no more than one tenth of a pixel in size, suspended in the inky blackness, alone in the vastness of the universe, harbouring the only sustained life as we know it. Every person or animal that has ever lived, or will live, must cohabit on this lonely speck of a planet.

We carry within us the wonders we seek without us.

Sir Thomas Browne

In 2009 Michael Massimino, an American astronaut, was on the space shuttle *Atlantis*. An important part of his mission was to carry out a complex repair to the Hubble Space Telescope. This involved leaving the comparative safety of the shuttle to spacewalk outside. Although not without its frustrations and delays, after about eight hours he succeeded in his task. Back in the airlock, while waiting to re-enter the shuttle, his commander told him he had about fifteen minutes before they would be ready for him and suggested that he go outside the airlock just to enjoy the view. So, he did, floating in space about 350 miles above the Earth and this is how Michael Massimino described what he saw:

> ... *the most magnificent thing I've ever seen. It's like looking into heaven. It's paradise ... and as I looked at the Earth, I also noticed I could turn my head and I could see the Moon and the stars and the Milky Way galaxy. I could see our universe. And I could turn back and I could see our beautiful planet. And that moment changed my relationship with the Earth. Because for me the Earth had always been a kind of*

safe haven ... but I realised (in that moment) it really wasn't. It really is its own 'spaceship'. And we've always been space travellers. All of us ... we're on this spaceship called Earth, amongst all the chaos of the universe, whipping around the Sun and around the Milky Way galaxy.

The magnitude of these words cannot be overstated. It is a concept of our understanding that can only be comprehended if we allow our minds to expand and our imaginations to soar.

Again, to quote Professor Stephen Hawking, '... it is only from the perspective of space ... in being able to look at planet Earth, that we can see our interconnectedness to the universe.'

Professor Hawking also echoed the words of Michael Massimino when he said, 'We are all time travellers, journeying together towards the future.' It is the sheer, awe-inspiring view of our complex planet when seen from space that should prompt us all to wonder at its origin, its authorship, its purpose and its future. Perhaps, more than ever, this awareness is a powerful affirmation of our responsibility to protect and look after its fragile environment for future generations.

I do not fear the explosive power of the atom bomb. What I fear is the explosive power of evil in the human heart.

Albert Einstein

There is a reason that so many – although not all – of the world's astronauts, who have been privileged to travel into space and look back on Earth, have returned changed, often more reflective, with an altered perspective on life.

Many embrace a new, or strengthened, faith in a higher being, or guiding hand.

... our planetary insignificance in the infinite vastness of space

Edgar Mitchell, one of the astronauts on the *Apollo 14* flight, famously said after his return, '... each astronaut went to the Moon as American citizens but returned as interplanetary citizens.' For Mitchell, this was an epiphany and he spent the rest of his life studying scientific consciousness.

James Irwin (*Apollo 15*) looking down on Earth from space saw, 'a living object ... so fragile, so delicate, that if you touched it with your finger it would crumble and fall apart. Seeing this has to change a man, has to make a man appreciate the creation of God.'

In this world, understanding gives rise to belief. But with things of the divine, it is belief that gives rise to understanding.

Erik Erikson (German/American psychologist)

As an analogy, think about holding just one single, perfectly spherical, grain of sand in the open palm of your hand, barely visible to the naked eye. Now gazing down at it, zoom right in close and try to imagine a whole miniaturized world of activity carrying on in an independently functioning, perfectly balanced, ecological planet, completely unaware of its precarious existence in being entirely dependent on you not discarding it with a brush of your hand.

Next, try looking at it from the point of view of any one of the tiny, tiny beings inhabiting this sub-lilliputian world who might stop whatever they are doing to look up in your direction to wonder what holds them in place, or even if 'you' are there at all and, if so, what power or force you might be and what, if any, name to give you.

Then ask yourself if you had delighted in the creation of this miniature life form, would you banish or forever extinguish any one of its inhabitants?

Maybe, but perhaps more likely not. Perpetual oblivion would be pointless and would render individual life as meaningless.

Hard though it might be to grasp, the reality is that our world – planet earth with all its billions of inhabitants – is far, far smaller than that grain of sand in your hand as it floats about in an infinite universe – the only planet among billions currently showing any form of life as we know it.

Until we can expand our minds to comprehend the infinitesimal smallness of our planet, it is easy to see how a narrow, Earth-centred perspective and limited scientific knowledge might lull us into believing that we have an explanation for everything – one that has no place for a higher guiding hand or purpose, in other words: no God.

Insignificant against the backdrop of the universe when viewed from space, the Earth with all its peoples, its triumphs and its tragedies, different, often bickering, religious beliefs and practices, can and must seem so inconsequential, even trivial. However, this view from space also reinforces the wonder and awe with which we should consider how such complex and finely-balanced mechanisms came into being – or perhaps always existed?

This brings us back to the central question of this book: accident or design? It is only after we, as individuals, decide which it is that the question is either answered, or many more questions arise and have to be explored.

Now, I have no idea if Michael Massimino is a man of faith or not, and I have no wish or intent to co-opt him into any such debate. I repeat only what he said of his experience.

However, it would not be wrong to suggest that often those who have been privileged to have extraordinary experiences such as his, are, at the very least, open to the possibility of the (divine) creator option – as opposed to the random cosmic accident one.

Similarly, it is interesting that a high proportion of people such as sailors, desert dwellers and travellers, who have observed the magnificence of the night sky in remote parts of the globe, have a deep spiritual awareness, or a belief in a guiding hand or higher power in their lives.

Of course, any of us – if we can get away from the star-dimming effects of light pollution – can lie on our backs and observe with wonder the enormity and depth of space as revealed on a starlit night. Doing so makes it hard not to question how what we are looking at came into being. The same is true of television documentaries about the wonders of modern astronomy that can now transport viewers far out into the almost incalculable expanse of the universe.

Everything we see is but a shadow cast by that which we do not see.

Dr Martin Luther King

When it comes to understanding the sheer size and age of our universe, it helps to get a little perspective. When the *Apollo 11* astronauts went to the Moon in July 1969, it took them more than three days to get there. Approaching thirty-six years later, when NASA's *New Horizons* mission to Pluto set off in January 2006, their unmanned spacecraft was travelling so fast it passed the Moon in just nine hours. Nevertheless, despite its truly incredible speed, it still took nine and a half years to travel the more than three billion miles to Pluto for its historic photographic flyby in July 2015.

Put the scale of the universe together with its age and the mind boggles. To illustrate this at a more mundane 'local' level here on Earth, it is worth thinking about what the stratification of the Grand Canyon in the US State of Arizona can show us. By studying its colourful layers, geologists have learned much about its history stretching back many millions of years. For example, it was once covered by shallow seas; was once lush with vegetation; and at one time was even flowing with lava.

Even the furore between science and religious doctrine that erupted when Nicolas Copernicus, the celebrated mediaeval astronomer, published his radical discovery that the Earth was merely another planet revolving around the Sun, rather than itself being the centre of the universe, did not (and does not) sit in conflict with the idea of intelligent design. More recent astronomical research and observation has, of course, shown the vast scale of this setting. It is interesting that, despite finding himself vilified for being at odds with church teachings, Copernicus never lost his faith and remained a believer in Christianity all his life.

On 21 December 1968, the *Apollo 8* astronauts Frank Borman, James Lovell and William Anders set off on a mission to orbit and photograph the Moon. They were able to beam their first pictures back to Earth on 24 December. So awed and overwhelmed were they by what they were seeing (the first humans ever to view the heavens in that way), and perhaps influenced by the significance of it being Christmas Eve, they felt inspired to offer a spiritual reading as a way of conveying to the millions of people watching and listening to the enormity of the occasion. The reading they chose was the opening verse of Genesis, the first book in the Bible. Taking turns, they read, 'In the beginning God created the heaven and earth.' This was not scripted or programmed into the mission; it was a spontaneous reaction to what they were seeing, and to the feelings it inspired in all three of them.

When the astronauts of *Apollo 11* went to the Moon they too felt compelled to express their profound feelings as witnesses to something so extraordinary and so other-worldly, that one of them was moved to say, 'Let's give thanks, each in his own way and own words.'

There is perhaps no better demonstration of the folly of human conceits than [witnessing] this distant image of our tiny world.

Carl Sagan (describing the image of Earth taken in 1990 by *Voyager I*, from a distance of six billion kilometres)

LOVE ACTUALLY

I will write love on the wind and let it blow all over the world.

Adapted from the writing of Sadako Sasaki (twelve-year-old Japanese girl who developed radiation leukaemia a decade after the atomic-bombing of Hiroshima)

It is in many ways restricting and confusing that in the English language we only have one word to express love, whether as an emotion or an expression of emphasis. By contrast the Greeks have four distinct words to express the different kinds of love: *philia* for love between friends, *storge* for love of family, *eros* for the love between two people (who have fallen in love) and *agape* for the broader love of humanity and our love for one another.

We talk about a life force as something primal and unstoppable, a force of such overwhelming magnitude as to be completely unimaginable and impossible for the human mind to comprehend; the only other force we know of equal magnitude is what we call love. Perhaps all the wonders of creation are themselves, collectively, just a triumphant expression of love – but this is a love so much greater than our general use of the word; fully embracing *philia*, *storge*, *eros* and *agape*, it is a force of love so all-powerful as to be able to bring order out of the chaos originating at the universe's beginnings. It is worth noting that love and faith are both risks that carry equally the promise of reward. Whether expressed as compassion or kindness, it is only love that has the power to change us for the better. If love imposes a burden, love also helps to carry it. Love can also inspire us to achieve extraordinary and powerful feats. In the well-known words of St John, often quoted at Christian and even non-Christian weddings, 'Perfect love drives out fear.' We need to believe in the positive power of love as opposed to the negative power of hate. To paraphrase an oft-quoted maxim: truth without love offends; love without truth deceives.

I have known hell, and I have also known love. Love was bigger.

Anne Lamott (author and past recipient
of a Guggenheim Fellowship)

With few exceptions, we all want to be loved; more than anything else in the world we crave love. The ancient Greek philosopher Aristotle remarked, 'No one would choose a friendless existence in exchange for having all the other things in the world'. Therefore, it would seem, we are all somehow designed and pre-programmed to give and receive love. But where does this completely universal emotion and need come from?

It is relevant here to take a moment to consider just what is love.

Not to be confused with lust or passion, love is the most powerful motivating force we know. It is also occasionally the most elusive and sometimes, if we are very lucky, enduring emotion. Love can include moments of intense connection between two people of such profound, personal, tender, all-consuming intimacy as to render all other senses meaningless and unnoticed. It is at moments such as this that awareness of time literally stops.

... the enduring purity of perfect love

It is this analogy of love 'stopping' time that may provide some small clue to the understanding of what Christians (and believers in other faiths) hope for in any afterlife. The early Christian theologian, Tertullian, stated, 'The confidence of Christians is the resurrection of the dead. Believing this enables them to live'.

Of course, love takes many forms, but in its purest it almost always carries the risk of great emotional vulnerability. As an expression of deep trust, love is often best communicated and experienced through the honesty of the eyes; there is good reason for the eyes to be called the windows to the soul.

Love is like glass, it looks so lovely but it's easy to shatter ... Life is a game for everyone, with love being its only true prize.

Athena Orchard, who died of cancer aged 12

Albert Einstein was once asked what a good subject would be to study for a doctoral thesis. His answer was surprising. He replied: 'Prayer, do a study on prayer; we need to know more about prayer.' A remarkable response from one of the world's greatest scientists!

As also shown in his writing, Einstein had a strong belief in humanity as an inseparable part of the One.

He wrote:

A human being is part of the whole ... what we refer to as the Universe ... we experience ourselves, our thoughts and feelings as something separate from the rest. A kind of optical delusion of consciousness. This delusion is a kind of prison for us, restricting us to our personal desires and to affection for a few persons nearest to us. Our task must be to free ourselves from the prison by widening our circle of compassion to the future embrace of all living creatures and the whole of nature and its beauty. The true value of a human being is determined by the measure and the sense in which they have obtained liberation from the self. We shall require a substantially new manner of thinking if humanity is to survive.

All shall be well, and all shall be well and all manner of things shall be well. For there is a force of love moving through the universe that holds fast and will never let us go.

Julian of Norwich (mediaeval anchoress, theologian and mystic)

The Opium of the People?

It has long been recognised that religion is a very powerful force; one which, in the wrong hands, can be as much a force for control and evil as, in the right hands, it can be for compassion and good.

However, as I have said earlier, this book does not set out to promote religion of any kind. In a way, what I am writing could be described as a precursor to any religious thought or practice; in other words, it is a starting point.

Ironically, unable to accept or overlook the many human failings of religion (hypocrisy, misogyny, racism, corruption, predatory exploitation of the weak, young or vulnerable) religion itself may be responsible for many people choosing a path of agnosticism, or even atheism.

This inevitably leads on to the question of whether the world's different religions may, or may not, have a helpful part to play. While religious extremism of any variety is at the very least deeply unpleasant, and at its worst fanatical, cruel and dangerous, it is too easy to focus on the many negatives in organised religion without stopping to consider the positives; to see only the flaws and none of the value. Given that we are all flawed individuals, with feet of clay, we would be wise to remember that, like almost any large institution, religion has both good and bad to offer. As fellow, fallible, human beings, while not condoning it, we must learn to be less judgmental and more understanding of the human weaknesses in those aiming – and often struggling, whether personally or collectively – to be, or to do, good.

Happily, in most cases, the good outweighs the bad – although, with some arguable justification, there will always be those who disagree with this!

So, for now, take a step back to a time before religion. But this raises another conundrum. Was there ever truly such a time? Perhaps evidence from the very earliest, primitive, yearnings for gods, spirits, shamans, sun worshippers and holy men by our prehistoric ancestors, is proof of the innate seeking for a meaning to life and its possible origins, hard-wired and deeply embedded within all of us.

Although there are almost certainly examples from all the major world religions, Augustine of Hippo from the Christian tradition must remain one of the most prominent. Born to a devoutly Christian mother (Monica) and a pagan father (Patricius), Augustine spent much of his early youth in the relentless pursuit of every hedonistic, sensual pleasure available: living with his mistress (who bore him a son), while revelling in his debauched lifestyle. The relevant point being that, after his conversion to Christianity at the age of twenty-eight, he subsequently admitted that all the while before his conversion he had, in fact, never stopped trying to find out 'where we come from, where we are going and how we can find the true meaning to life'. The same essential questions almost everyone feels prompted to ask themselves at some point in their lives.

Anyone who has studied enough history will already know that myriad religions, beliefs and practices have come and gone, more often than not waxing and waning in accordance with the manipulative intentions of political or religious leaders.

Jesus came to save us from religion.

Paul Tillich

A wise hermit once wrote, 'The one who knows does not say, and the one who says does not know' – his point being that those who write, read, study and speak endlessly on matters of religion often miss what is revealed through quiet thought.

The essential problem with religious fundamentalists is that they focus on hate rather than love. Hatred masquerading as religion is as objectionable and hollow as it is insulting. With less of a dogmatic approach, and a great deal more humility amongst all religions, there may well be a role for religion in general to help guide scientific research as it gropes for answers to the biggest of all questions under consideration here.

Religion should always resist any temptation to be political or manipulative for its own purposes. Christian religions also need to be brave in considering and accepting change.

They need to play their part in this change as well; where necessary, by being more adventurous in their approach to exploring science, and more trusting in people's awareness of their frailties, flaws and weaknesses.

Mentioned three times in different gospel accounts, permission to implement change would appear to have been explicitly given by Jesus himself, when he said directly to Simon Peter, 'And I will give to thee the keys to the kingdom of heaven and whatsoever thou shalt bind on earth shall be bound in heaven and whatsoever shall be loosed on earth shall be loosed in heaven.'

Dietrich Bonhoeffer, the German Lutheran Pastor who, as an eminent theologian, spoke out and stood against Nazism in the Second World War when other religious leaders remained silent, came to advocate for a more involved 'religion-less' Christianity that would show its willingness to confront these kinds of crises.

Dr Martin Luther King Jnr, a man of deep Christian faith and practice, famously declared, 'Any religion that professes to be concerned about the souls of men and is not concerned about the slums that damn them, the economic conditions that strangle them and the social conditions that cripple them, is a spiritually moribund religion awaiting burial.'

Paraphrasing the wise words of theologian Ronald Rolheiser, if religion of any persuasion is to be helpful it should not be one of condemnation but one embracing brokenness and loving forgiveness in not teaching how to live so much as teaching how to live again . . . and again . . . and again . . .

Preach the gospel – using words if you must.

St Francis of Assisi (13th-century founder
of the Franciscan order)

Keeping Faith

> Nothing obscures the face of God quite so effectively as religion; it can be a substitute for God himself.
>
> Martin Buber (Austrian Jewish theologian and philosopher)

Faith is sometimes hard to identify through the fog of religion which, like all fog, comes in degrees of impenetrability.

While an honest religion sincerely practised can be an enabler, faith and religion remain two separate entities. It is possible to have faith without religion, but, in its essence, pointless to have religion without faith – apart from those who regard churchgoing solely as a comforting and reassuring ritual. As someone wisely noted, 'Going to church doesn't make you a person of faith any more than standing in a garage makes you a car'.

Unfortunately, religion can complicate and sometimes even obscure the essentially simple message of faith. That said, it is important not to undermine or devalue the role that a healthy approach to religion can play in the establishment or development of faith. Always remembering that living with faith involves living with uncertainties.

There is a misconception that faith is a worthless crutch relied on by the weak and weak-minded. But what is weak? One of the smallest, least significant seeds is that of the mustard plant. However, once planted it has the strength and power to break through concrete. In the same way, the hidden forces of microbial life silently and, little by little, influence almost every action and reaction in biological evolution.

Being a true atheist involves living life without the sort of hope held by a believer or agnostic, a concept that, in all probability, gets progressively bleaker as old age and infirmity creep up on us.

Because the opposite of faith must be certainty, albeit a grim certainty, it is self-evident that faith must encompass doubt. So, if faith and doubt are simply two sides of the same coin, faith and hope are first cousins.

Faith in a purpose or an afterlife is not an insurance policy and does not seek to escape from the otherwise grim reality of nothingness. Instead, faith conquers the meaninglessness and far more illogical acceptance of creation as merely a random accident. Having something to live for is of almost equal importance to having enough to live on. Faith turns the prospect of a hopeless end into one filled with the expectation of endless hope.

If – and for some that may be a big if – you decide there is a hopeful something, rather than a bleak nothing, it may be time to go on and explore, with due care and caution, the healthier realms of honest religion and its relationship with honest science.

But, that is not the purpose of this book. When it comes to religion, I leave it to you to pursue your own enquiries, ask your own questions and evaluate the answers you arrive at.

In faith there is enough light for those who want to believe and enough shadow to blind those who don't.

Blaise Pascal

Carl Sagan was a brilliant and very likeable scientist who had the gift of being a good communicator and educator. A deep thinker, Sagan made weighty scientific matters exciting and understandable to all.

Although Sagan struggled with the concept of any form of afterlife, with his customary humility and open-mindedness, he was probably more agnostic than atheist – a fact confirmed by his wife, Ann Druyan, after his death. Sagan's definition of an atheist is an interesting one that demonstrates his humility on the subject: 'An atheist has to know a lot more than I know. An atheist is someone who knows there is no God'.

Sagan also said, 'Sceptical scrutiny is the means, in both science and religion, by which deep thoughts can be winnowed from deep nonsense.'

Imagination will often carry us to worlds that never were. But without it we go nowhere.

Carl Sagan

WE ARE STARDUST?

> Words strain,
> Crack and sometimes break, under the burden,
> Under the tension, slip, slide, perish,
> Decay with imprecision, will not stay in place,
> Will not stay still. Shrieking voices
> Scolding, mocking, or merely chattering,
> Always assail them.
>
> T S Eliot

When addressing the inadequacy of language (above) Eliot voices the concern that thoughts committed to paper often fail to convey the same meaning they did as ideas in the mind. Language is slippery and, unfortunately, written words can be limiting and a constraint on our thoughts. And this does not allow for changes to the meaning of words that happen over time. The straightforward fact (or, without the initial 'f', the not so straightforward act) of creation is so mind-boggling to most of us that the frequently misused adjective 'awesome' is wholly inadequate, even when used in its proper context.

Let us take the human body as an example. Depending on how it is calculated, there are somewhere between 15 and 40 trillion cells in every person – all of them interconnected and working together. As if that were not amazing enough, the human body is composed of seven billion, billion, billion atoms, ninety-nine per cent of which are constituted of just six elements: oxygen, carbon, hydrogen, nitrogen, calcium and phosphorus. We are all but temporary gatherings of stardust.

> **The nitrogen in our DNA, the calcium in our teeth, the iron in our blood, the carbon in our apple pies, were all made in the interiors of collapsing stars. We are all made of starstuff.**
>
> Carl Sagan

Then there is the amazing microbial world of the currently fashionable gut bacteria, the vital importance of which to our general health we are only just beginning to understand and get to grips with.

To take a wider view of the life on Earth, although from a scientific perspective the familiar process of photo-synthesis may be viewed as a relatively simple, elegant, chemical reaction, it is nevertheless fundamental to all forms of life. In fact, almost all life is ultimately reliant on photosynthesis for its survival.

The same is true of the never-ending cycle of the seasons as they meld from one to the other. Their rhythm and regularity are so familiar that we take their year-round passage for granted. But that seasonal cycle is vital to the lives of virtually every living thing on Earth.

The inescapable fact (these being thin on the ground!) is that these processes had to start somewhere. And this brings us right back to the 'dilemma'. Did they originate from a 'seed' or 'thought' of creation planted by a divine creator?

... a journey of wondrous scientific discovery

Albeit a longshot for many, this concept is arguably nothing like such a longshot as accepting the very beginning of life as the spontaneous, self-planted 'seed' of an evolutionary process. There is an almost overwhelming weight of evidence to suggest that the world is not just a machine, ticking over like a watch. It is more like a unity, directed by an infinite mind, which some people choose to call God.

> **… every atom in a human was made in a star. We are all made of this stuff, and when we look into the night sky and see starlight it is natural to wonder how it began.**
>
> Professor Richard Ellis, University College London

Looking with faith and hope beyond what happens in our tangible, visible, world can suggest that there is an invisible world hidden behind the veil of what we can see and sense. Incomparably more important than what happens in the visible world of the senses is the truth of the invisible world. Indeed, a definition of faith is, 'Being sure of what we hope for and certain of what we cannot see.' Living with a sense of hope is much more than mere wishful thinking. Hope has the power to change everything.

Helen Keller, the famous American teacher who, against all the odds at the time, overcame the joint disabilities of being totally blind and deaf, and who went on to become one of the last century's greatest humanitarians, claimed that blindness gave her 'a deep sense that things seen are temporal and things unseen are eternal.' We live by faith and not by sight.

> **Faith sees the invisible, believes the unbelievable and receives the impossible.**
>
> Corrie ten Boom

To Mingle with the Universe

It is a popular belief that we know with scientific certainty that everything, absolutely everything, must have a beginning and an end – including life itself.

If this is so, it raises the questions, 'What happened before that beginning of life? And what allowed, enabled or designed that beginning?' I suspect that the answers would strongly hint at what, if anything, might be expected after the end.

As an alternative to this, some scientists have not been afraid to hypothesise that for all we know the universe could one day be proved to be eternal – without a beginning or end. This might suggest there would be no need for, or never to have been a need for, a creator (or God).

Surprisingly, this position is not incompatible with many religious beliefs which have always acknowledged God as eternal. The words in some versions of the Christian Credo exemplify this: 'God before time began'. Nor is it incompatible to consider evolution within the position of an eternal universe.

God is like an infinite circle whose centre is everywhere and whose circumference is nowhere.

St Augustine of Hippo (4th/5th-century Roman African Manichaean Christian theologian)

Way back in the sixteenth century, although at a time when it must be acknowledged our understanding of the world and science was much more primitive, Blaise Pascal posited that human beings bet with their lives that God either exists or does not; this is still referred to as 'Pascal's Wager.' In simple terms it runs as follows: if you live your life in the belief or hope that God exists, you have little to lose and everything to gain in an as yet unknown eternity. Whereas, if you live your life without any such belief or hope, you ultimately have everything to lose in any such eternity. One way (of living) is for now, the other is forever. In what is essentially a one-way bet, it could be said that, if 'the battle' is for the mind of the agnostic, this should make little or no difference to the confirmed atheist but mean a great deal to the believer who has faith and wants to share it.

Pascal presented his famous wager as a much more methodical equation of probabilities with a supporting mathematical formula for which he was widely criticised, largely because of a misunderstanding of the idea he was putting forward. The wager does not conclude with a QED at the end of its mathematical submission. It was merely meant to show that logical reasoning cannot support faith or the lack thereof.

In his *Pensées* (published after his death) Pascal states, 'Belief in God does not depend upon rational evidence, no matter which position'. He did not offer the wager as any proof of God's existence, but rather as a necessary pragmatic decision which is 'impossible to avoid' for any living person. He went on to argue that abstaining from making a wager is not an option, and that 'reason is incapable of divining the truth'. Therefore, according to his thesis, a decision over whether to believe in the existence of God must be made by 'considering the consequences of either possibility' – or perhaps on a balance of probabilities?

While not accepting God in any traditional sense, pantheism believes that in nature all is one with God, and therefore that nature is God and is indivisible from God. Pantheism also holds that we humans are part of the one interconnected whole.

The seventeenth-century pantheist philosopher Baruch Spinoza reached the conclusion that 'All is one', and he described reality (by which he meant what exists) in terms of 'One Substance'. Therefore, in accepting nature as God, does pantheism not go a long way towards belief in a starting point, or intelligent design?

Spinoza was preceded in this way of thinking by the ancient Greek philosophers and mathematicians Parmenides and his young disciple Zeno, who espoused the doctrine of the existence of 'the one' indivisible reality, without being able to go further in stating what 'the one' might actually be.

So, the universe must be a rational being and the nature which permeates and embraces all things must be endowed with reason in its highest form. And, so, God and the world of Nature must be one and all the life of the world must be contained within the being of God.

Marcus Tullius Cicero (1st-century BC Roman orator, statesman, and man of letters)

During an interview about his life, a young man of strong faith, who had been wheelchair-bound following a serious accident as a seven-year-old, surprised everyone by staunchly declaring his belief that 'God was fair'. Incredulous, the interviewer asked the young man if he thought what had happened to him was fair? Smiling, the young man replied, 'That depends on your view as to whether, or not, this life is all there is. This is for now, but consider the very briefness of anyone's lifespan. God has all of eternity to make this up to me. One day everything will be put right.' This young man was completely confident in his ability to see beyond the limitations and finite nature of this world.

This is not intended to simplify, sugar coat, denigrate or in any way devalue those who may feel very differently over such dreadful, life-changing misfortunes. Anger, rage, resentment, complete loss of faith or hope, contemplation of suicide, are all understandable and legitimate reactions.

In summary, let me turn to the noted pastor Jim Penner, whose words on this subject I paraphrase as:

So, my atheist friend – and I do mean friend – you say there is no God? Yet there is no Hollywood special effects house that can even come close to matching the majesty of a thunderstorm. No medical engineer who can recreate the human brain or breathe life into a new-born. No physicist who can hurl comets across the sky. No marine biologist who can create a whale or calm the seas. No entomologist who can transform a caterpillar into a butterfly. No medical technician who can balance the earth's atmosphere with just the right blend of oxygen. No Wall Street wizard who can fill the earth with silver and gold or turn coal into diamonds. No meteorologist who can create or stop a hurricane, or fill the western sky with the brilliant colours of a spectacular sunset.

Think about that and ask yourself again if you can be quite so sure in your atheism?

On the Origin of …?

There is an argument that claims the two greatest days of your life are the day you were born and the day you find out why.

While it shouldn't be controversial or divisive, in the end the question under discussion in this book comes down to a binary decision: either there is some purpose to our existence, or there is not. If you choose the former, it is OK to have doubt; as I mentioned earlier, faith both addresses and transcends doubt. But if you choose the latter, any doubt becomes self-defeating and pointless as you will have chosen certainty instead – albeit a grim certainty.

Of course, the concept of intelligent design does not of itself automatically guarantee an afterlife, or any form of reincarnation in this world or the next. Nor does this book make any claim to the certainty of an afterlife, beyond the meaning such an eventuality would give to its essential proposition.

Hope and fear cannot occupy the same space at the same time. We have to invite one of them to stay.

Maya Angelou (20th-century American poet and civil rights activist)

Humanism and pantheism share a common problem, in that neither go far enough in fully addressing the question of whether, and if so by whom or what, the 'natural' creative force was first established. Was it a cosmic accident? Or was it, after all, perhaps created?

Straightforward atheism is at least unambiguous on this point. Of course, in accepting the possibility of a creative force one must also accept that all life forms (including human life) belong to that creative force, rather than to the nebulous, random action of a cosmic accident – to which one would owe nothing.

Another problem faced by all three persuasions is that they tend to overlook the manifest unfairness of life. Is this too simply random good or bad luck? Or does it have a purpose we cannot know or see at present?

When contemplating the possibility of a higher power or universal mind, many people struggle with the cruelty of life and question how a benign, all-loving deity could allow such imbalances in a world that same deity created. In other words, why do bad things happen to good people? Something for which, beyond speculation, we do not have an answer.

It is unfortunate that the word 'miracle' has become inextricably rooted in a religious context, because 'miracle' stems from the Latin word for 'an object of wonder'. Thus, in its secular sense, it is true to say that a miracle is not contrary to nature; only to what we know about nature.

Miracles have everything to do with faith or, if you prefer, spiritual belief. If, after all, life is just a huge cosmic accident, there is nothing more to be said – and there is no need for the confirmed atheist to read further! But it would be worth asking how many atheists still harbour superstitions?

Faith is not a soft option, but a state of mind or a gift available to all who are prepared to work for it, and even struggle and suffer at times. Perhaps the need to persevere with faith leads some people to opt for the path of a passive agnosticism or atheism; intellectual laziness avoids the struggle of addressing the complexities behind the concept of intelligent design. So often the inclination to talk about life's profound questions is obscured or avoided in today's world.

True humility is not thinking less of yourself, it is thinking of yourself less.

C S Lewis

Of course, many people – perhaps even a majority in some Western countries – are agnostic.

It is interesting that the list of famous agnostics from all fields of endeavour is considerably longer than that of confirmed atheists. Many agnostics will quite likely adopt the ostrich response to the issues under consideration here, by simply avoiding any thought that might force a decision. Although there are beliefs and practices, Buddhism for example, that are technically atheist in as much as they do not espouse the concept of an original creator, atheism does not satisfactorily address how the world and life as we know it came into being.

At the same time, it would be a mistake for any subscribers to a strictly fundamentalist view of creation to take comfort from this. The flaw in the likelihood of a completely literal Adam and Eve can be seen in almost all artistic paintings or depictions which clearly show them with navels. Rigorous science cannot afford the luxury of artistic naivety, however appealing.

I used the word 'possibility' earlier in relation to there being some sort of original creator. For the purposes of this book it should of course be the probability – or certainty – of such an entity (or deity if you prefer). In no way does evolution preclude this belief; arguably, in fact, evolution enhances it! Perhaps it is this that explains why roughly fifty per cent of scientists describe themselves as having some sort of belief in a higher power, or external influence.

It was not very long ago that the pioneering astronomer Sir Fred Hoyle enraged his atheist peers by declaring that he had reached the conclusion that there was a greater likelihood of intelligent design at work in the creation of life on Earth, rather than it being the consequence of a cosmic accident.

Sir Fred, who formulated the theory of stellar nucleosynthesis and rejected the Big Bang theory (but was also apparently an ardent atheist for most of his life), used a telling analogy to make his point. If life on Earth was a cosmic accident, it would be equivalent to a tornado rushing through a scrapyard and assembling a fully working Boeing 747 aircraft as it passed.

Sir Fred Hoyle was not going so far as to claim the existence of a God in any religious sense, but he felt compelled by the rigorous honesty he had always applied to his scientific work to follow the evidence as far as anyone can. He also famously said, 'There is a coherent plan to the universe, though I don't know what it is a plan for'.

To know that we know what we know, and to know that we do not know what we do not know, that is true knowledge.

Nicolas Copernicus

Another eminent scientist, Lord Rees President of the Royal Society, proffered this contribution, 'Let me say that I don't see any conflict between science and religion [in this sense the implication being faith]. I go to church as many other scientists do. I share with most religious people [people of faith] a sense of mystery and wonder at the universe.'

Of the three simple lessons astronaut Nicole Stott brought back from her journey into space, the most important was her realisation that ultimately there is only one border that matters and that is the thin blue line of atmosphere that blankets us all. This makes national frontiers and the territorial whims of political leaders seem trivial to the point of being laughable in their narrow-mindedness.

G K Chesterton made an honest point when, in writing a letter to *The Times* in response to the topic 'What is wrong with the human race', he replied simply, 'Dear Sir, I am. Yours sincerely, G K Chesterton'.

With the recent advent of popular 'genetic testing' the whole concept of race should be redefined. In the opinion of Anne Wojcicki, the founder and CEO of 23andme Genetic Testing, 'Almost everyone is more diverse than they realise. You may be culturally part of a group, but you discover your genetic ancestry was different'. It is that that makes her feel the whole debate surrounding immigration should be looked at differently. She goes on to say, 'It opens your eyes to the fact you have DNA in common with people who were not brought up at all like you. Genetically we are all very similar, if not geographically, and every genetic mutation – blue eyes, lighter skins – tells a story about how we adapt for survival.'

This life is a battleground, but it is not the end.

Bear Grylls OBE (British adventurer and
former SAS serviceman)

A more down-to-earth example is well illustrated in the close, even friendly, cooperation between the multinational group of scientists and researchers – many from countries ideologically and politically opposed to each other – who are involved in the Antarctic Survey mission. Living as they do in one of the most inhospitable and isolated places on Earth encourages them to appreciate their common humanity.

As the world's natural resources come under increasing pressure, the experiences forged among this disparate scientific community tell us just how pressing and important it is that we all – world leaders and influencers in particular – need to overcome narrow nationalistic, territorial preconceptions and prejudices. Unfortunately, most such leaders succumb to the temptation to see leadership positions as the means of exercising power rather than the opportunity to serve.

There is a word, *ubantu*, taken from the South African Nguni collection of languages, which, translates loosely to mean 'I am well if you are well', thus conveying a sense of interconnectedness, of interdependence and human belonging which is fundamental to human spiritual need.

We must all work together to raise our sights and up our game in considering how we peacefully co-exist and how we cooperate in protecting the planet we share. In doing so, it behoves us not to ignore, but to consider, the origin of the life we are all privileged to enjoy here.

All men are caught in an inescapable network of
mutuality, tied in a single garment of destiny.

Dr Martin Luther King Jnr

... the necessity of friendly cooperation for survival

In the same way that we should celebrate the distinction of individual nationalities and cultures which add so much vibrancy and interest to life, we should also truly value the symbiotic, interdependent nature of the ecosystems of the planet. They, like us, are finely balanced in maintaining the equilibrium of life. Together, we are a perfect work exemplified by the extraordinary biodiversity found on earth.

Apart from being able to inspire people with courage and fortitude, genuinely great leaders have the shared qualities of focus, authenticity, compassion, generosity and humility. They also have big visions which make them unafraid to aim for the stars.

Although the whole climate change debate is a separate issue, mostly unrelated to the purpose of this book, it is just worth noting that there is something of an irony over the action begun in 2018 by the then fifteen-year-old Swedish schoolgirl Greta Thunberg – a controversial figure to some, considered precocious, unrealistic and ill-informed by many – who fearlessly campaigned over the urgent need to recognise and grapple with the devastating effects of climate change. Her diminutive physique did not hold her back when addressing world leaders; and she showed no sign of being intimidated when speaking truth to power.

Greta Thunberg cannot ever have imagined it – and would most certainly never have wanted her wish to come true in this way – but the worldwide coronavirus shutdown brought about such a drastic reduction in global carbon emissions that it could have contributed to some nations' ability to attain what otherwise might have been overambitious climate-control targets.

Although, from an economic point of view, the Covid-19 crisis was clearly just about the worst possible way to achieve these goals, it did prove to be a catalyst for ushering in fresh growth opportunities as the world is forced to adapt and change to new greener technologies.

To put everything in balance is good; to put everything in harmony is better.

Victor Hugo

In 2019, one of the laureates for the Templeton Prize (mentioned earlier), Marcelo Gleiser, was interviewed on BBC's Radio 4's *Sunday* programme and stated that 'atheism is inconsistent with scientific method', adding that in his opinion there is no conflict between science and faith.

Professor Gleiser, the Professor of Physics and Astronomy at prestigious Dartmouth College in New Hampshire, USA, is a theoretical physicist, cosmologist and a leading proponent of the view that 'science, philosophy and spirituality are complementary expressions of humanity's need to embrace mystery and the unknown.' Although raised in a devout Jewish family, his rigorous academic training has led him to have a sort of de-conversion experience from organised religion and he has instead become a self-confessed agnostic.

Nevertheless, he is a firm believer in there having been something more than a cosmic accident at the start of life. Similarly, the twice Nobel Prize-winning scientist and physicist Marie Curie eventually reached a position of agnosticism after abandoning her Roman Catholic upbringing. In aligning herself with an approach towards science and scientific discovery that any confident religion would do well to embrace, she famously said 'nothing in life is to be feared – only understood'.

Following the justifiable excitement when the existence of the Higgs Boson Particle was confirmed in 2012 as a result of the Atlas experiment at CERN, its director general, particle physicist Fabiola Gianotti, spontaneously declared, 'Thank you nature' – for which she was applauded by many.

This of course only demonstrates the depth of understanding we should accede to nature when contemplating the universe. Seeking such an understanding neither proves nor disproves the concept of a beginning, or any form of intelligent design; but it may, perhaps, lead to yet another tantalising indicator of there being something.

The soul has been given its own ears to hear things the mind does not understand.

Rumi

Following many years of meticulous research in which over 2,000 scientists worked together to decipher and map the three billion 'letters' or symbols that make up the human genome, one of the foremost of these scientists reached a conclusion about the beginnings of life, summed up in the following statement, 'I cannot see how nature could have created itself. Only a supernatural force that is outside space and time could have done that'.

A while ago, a fascinating programme called *Something Wild* aired on New Hampshire Public Radio, in which the true reason behind the annual variation in the acorn crop was explained. It is often believed that a year producing a bumper crop of acorns is a reliable indicator of a hard winter to come. To believe that the oak tree would be capable of 'knowing' such things would be an amazing enough example by itself, but the process is in fact far cleverer and more complex than that.

… the mystery of the fluctuating annual acorn harvest

It seems that the size of the acorn crop is related to what is known as masting: any nuts, seeds or fruit that trees produce, which in turn provide essential food for animals. The quantity of acorns from an oak tree follows a boom or bust cycle which means the size of the acorn crop varies from year to year. The fascinating thing is that, over time, evolution has favoured those oak trees that most prominently demonstrate this boom or bust phenomenon.

Research has shown that this keeps acorn-consuming animals off-balance – which is a good thing.

If the size of the acorn crop was the same every year, there would always be enough animal consumers of acorns and few, if any, acorns would survive to become new oak trees. But, by producing very few acorns for a year or two, oak trees effectively starve the animals, thereby greatly reducing their populations. Then, when the cunning oak tree has a boom year and there are not enough animals left to eat all the acorns, some of the uneaten acorns survive to become trees.

Take a moment to consider just how the oak tree 'knows' that it needs to do this and marvel at this one small instance of the complexities within nature.

Or consider the giant redwood sequoia trees of Northern California and how they propagate. Of the three known ways – through the agency of beetles and squirrels, or as a result of forest fires – fires are the most effective. The hard cones of the sequoia tree, that hold the seeds, dry out in the heat from a forest fire, releasing their seeds. These seeds need clear ground and sunlight to germinate and prosper, conditions that are fortuitously provided by the clearing action of the fire. These give the young sequoia seedlings a head start with clear ground, open to sunlight, for several years before competing vegetation re-establishes itself.

An equally extraordinary example from the world of insects would be the flight of the dragonfly. The bio-mechanical design and development of a dragonfly's wings allows the front pair to operate independently from the back pair.

And of course, the humble bumble bee continues to fly happily about unaware that its wing design and the ratio of its body-to-wing-size means that it defies all the known laws of aerodynamics!

Or the ant colony, where a highly complex, sophisticated hierarchical system for living in such dense, close quarters, follows established rules of hygiene and solicitous nursing care that would be the envy of any human society!

That is before recognising the mind-blowing, unseen, but vital influence that the myriad different forms of fungi play in all of nature and all of our lives. From use in medicine and healing, combatting viral infections to the environmental degradation of plastics and other man-made substances, including radioactive contamination.

In the plant world, the rare and secretive Kadupul Flower, which can be found in the southern parts of North America, but is primarily native to Sri Lanka, is possibly the most expensive flower in the world. However, it would be better described as genuinely priceless. The almost mystically enchanting Kadupul Flower is so frail and shy that it blooms just before midnight and is over and gone before daybreak. It has a sweet fragrance, hailed for its soothing effect. The Native American Indians held that if you prayed while the flower was in bloom, your prayers would be answered.

> It is the common wonder of all men how, among so
> many millions of faces, there should be none
> exactly alike.
>
> Sir Thomas Browne

Without going into too much technical detail, if I were to choose just one example (out of millions) from human biology, I would opt for the vestibular system: a three-dimensional, semi-circular canal apparatus in every human head, the primary purpose of which is to detect and compensate for rotational movements in any direction. Using a network of very fine hair cells and a tiny membrane, weighted down with protein-calcium carbonate granules, all imbedded within our ears, it is a marvel of biological engineering and perfectly controls so much of our movement, vision, balance, spatial orientation and sense of gravity. Could such a delicate component of the human and animal world really have come about by chance?

The seemingly intuitive connection between animals and humans merits inclusion here as further revelation of a creative force at work.

Several examples caught my attention when researching this book, the first of which took place in 2000, when Kevin Hines tried to kill himself by jumping off the Golden Gate Bridge in San Francisco Bay. After he plunged into the water a sea lion kept him afloat until the Coast Guard arrived and rescued him.

In 2014, a pod of dolphins circled four lifeguards on a training swim off the coast of New Zealand and began slapping the water with their fins, alerting the lifeguards to the proximity of a great white shark.

In 1996 a gorilla named Binti Jua rescued a three-year-old boy who fell into her enclosure at a zoo in Illinois. She guarded him from other gorillas before carrying him to safety. In 2005 a pride of lions in Ethiopia are credited with protecting a twelve-year-old girl who had been dumped and abandoned by kidnappers.

... protected by innocence

Perhaps the most remarkable example of animal/ human understanding is related by Bear Grylls in his inspirational book *Soul Fuel*, in which he refers to Koko – a gorilla that was, against all prevailing wisdom, taught sign language, eventually learning more than 1,000 words with an ability to understand nearly 2,000 spoken words. When asked by a journalist for the meaning of life, she signed 'People be polite – people have goodness'.

Be polite. Have goodness. It's funny how so much of science and the natural world are intertwined with humanity, instinctively working in harmony.

What senses are at work here between the animal and human world and where do these instincts come from? Perhaps it is true that each small task of everyday life is part of the total harmony of the universe.

When it comes to arriving at a simple answer to this biggest of all questions, 'What is the meaning of life?', Koko may be closer to the truth than we realise. If you allow yourself to consider the possibility of an intelligent designer, you would have to acknowledge that each of us was created without any input, knowledge or consent of our own. With consciousness and free will, however, it may be that our actions and how we live our lives will have a bearing on determining our futures in another dimension.

We're not alone in this universe. We're not on some pointless mission that makes no sense and has no destination.

Bear Grylls

Go into a graveyard and look at any grave, old or new. Consider the life of the person buried there. Did that life have any meaning at all, or was it too just a meaningless part of a cosmic accident?

Alternatively, consider that we might be standing on the shoulders of those countless lives that have gone before, those brave young men and women killed in many wars, or other people who have lived long and fulfilled lives.

Do we ever stop to give any thought, or thanks, to our forebears for their part in our lives? For their life experiences, energies, sacrifices, joys and difficulties that may all play a tiny part in shaping who we are today? Include in this evidence of the extraordinary sophistication of earlier civilisations that date back thousands of years.

If I have seen further than others it is by standing on the shoulders of giants.

Sir Isaac Newton (17th/18th-century mathematician, astronomer and physicist)

It is interesting to reflect that almost all humans seem to have been hardwired from the beginning with an innate awareness of good and evil, often waging a titanic battle within them. Even the best of us can grow weary from this conflict and succumb to temptations that go against that part of our being that would be good. The popularity of such epic films as *Star Wars* and *The Lord of the Rings* are testimony of this. From where, however, did this conscience originate? Although usually explained away with the unsatisfactory catch-all answer 'It's just human nature', it still leaves the unanswered question, 'But where does this force of human nature come from?'

The question, then, is who or what is capable of such an expression of a love so powerful that good triumphs in the end? The dilemma we all face is in having to decide!

Interestingly, within Christianity, it is often stated that God is love. It may be argued in this context that all of creation is an expression of love, and therefore that faith without love is merely ideology.

For all our supposed cleverness, we human beings (with a few very rare exceptions) are really just stumbling around in our own stupidity. We blindly grope our way through life in the primitive, self-centred selfishness of the here and now, unable to focus on the big picture of a distant future, or even learn from a distant past.

Having decided on the greater likelihood of there being a creator, it leaves little room for secularism and must therefore lead towards belief.

So, to summarise, we are faced with two options: choosing one and having the grim satisfaction of 'knowing' the outcome is to live life without any hope for a future in the hereafter; or choosing the other and living life in the full expectant joy of hope of what may lie beyond death. And it is with a continual hope most of us live out our daily lives anyway!

However, to be effective, this hope must lead on to belief. Hope by itself is vague, lazy and passive; whereas belief is dynamic, optimistic and positive. Thus, hope should be a precursor to belief.

The line separating good and evil passes, not through states, nor through classes, nor between political parties ... but right through every human heart – and through all human hearts.

Aleksandr Solzhenitsyn

Sometimes we need to allow ourselves to think in terms of a much, much bigger picture – to allow our minds to expand and imagine on a scale seldom taught or encouraged by mainstream education; in short, to wonder freely, without intellectual borders or barriers.

Curiosity and wonder are the prism through which we can discern the gift of wisdom. If one allows one's mind that same perspective enjoyed by astronauts such as Michael Massimino and Tim Peake, it is harder not to accept the hand of an intelligent designer at work, than it is to think of it as an arbitrary set of circumstances coming together by pure chance.

The beginning of wisdom is wonder.

Aristotle

Although he may perhaps lean more towards humanism or pantheism, it is interesting that world famous natural historian Sir David Attenborough, when acknowledging that there might in fact be a God, once said 'nature wastes nothing'. There are myriad examples of this being true, so doubtless he is correct.

But, if this is the case, it raises the question of what happens to the enormous repository of knowledge and information collected in human brains throughout many lifetimes. Where does it all go when we die? Is this an example of nature disproving Sir David's theory through a devastating act of the most incredible wastage?

Or, as is more likely the case, is Sir David again quite right and, if so, might this accumulated knowledge re-emerge in some unforeseen alternative metaphysical dimension? The very circle of life embraced by many in Asian cultures!

If you watch how nature deals with adversity, continually renewing itself, you cannot help but learn from it.

Bernie Siegel (American writer, doctor and philosopher)

It is easy to be persuaded by the fact that throughout history, particularly in recent history, some of our very brightest and cleverest minds have been atheists, humanists, pantheist or existentialists. Some of them have often been forceful in their derision of anyone professing belief in the concept of an author of life. The French philosopher Jean Paul Sartre, an intellectual giant and considered by many to be the father of modern existentialism (a rather depressing and fatalistic philosophy which dismisses our very existence as ultimately meaningless and therefore empty) said, 'Everything has been figured out – except how to live.'

To counteract this, it is worth stopping to consider that just as many equally intelligent and clever minds, some of the greatest that ever lived, have accepted the stronger likelihood of the presence of a higher power in their lives, giving them a reason to live and a reason to die – even though that reason may not yet be fully known. It is tempting to speculate that at least among some in the former group the confusion between faith and religion raises its head again.

Eventually all things fall into place. Until then, laugh at the confusion, live for the moments, and know everything happens for a reason.

Albert Schweitzer

It is customary in many criminal trials for the jury to be influenced by what is sometimes called overwhelming circumstantial evidence, as opposed to conclusive evidence or proof. By most worldly measures, the existence or non-existence of a creative power can neither be 'conclusively' proved nor disproved. Thus, we are left to consider and examine the circumstantial evidence.

Each of us must draw our own conclusions. It is the proposition of this book that the circumstantial evidence for the existence of a higher power is indeed overwhelming.

This should be a reason for joy and celebration, not the rigours and guilt of a dry, excessive religiosity; the crux of the matter is not the force of religion, but the joint powers of faith and love. That higher power, that some choose to call God, is essentially love; something all religions would do well to remember and act upon as a guiding light.

In everyone there sleeps a sense of life lived according to love.

Philip Larkin (English poet)

Although we may not start at the same point in pondering the two choices we all must face in life, if you finally fall on the side of faith in something bigger than we are – while allowing for some moments of doubtful stumbling along the way – that faith will likely grow and become stronger. It is at this point we can then decide if a religion can or needs to play any part in its development.

Collective acts of worship often have value in reinforcing this faith, in the same way that if you try to start a fire by lighting one stick, it is likely the flame will die, but try lighting a bundle of sticks and you will soon have a merry blaze. Or, as the wise African proverb says, 'If you want to go fast, go alone; but if you want to go far, go together.'

This book is not intending to disavow religion. It is trying instead to take a step back from religion, to focus on what the essential beginning of faith in a divine creator might be.

> **Faith is not a guarantee of safe passage against life's adversities. It does not impose any obligations upon God – only upon us human beings.**
>
> Anonymous

IN
CONCLUSION

Throughout history there are many examples of how 'experts', from doctors, highly-educated economists and financial experts, to scientifically-trained weather forecasters, have been proved radically wrong in their pronouncements.

Although almost certainly apocryphal, one favourite and often quoted example is that of Tom Watson, one-time president of IBM, who, opining on the future of the computer in 1943, is reputed to have said, 'I think there is a world market for maybe five computers'.

A more reliable example of expert hubris would be that of Irving Fisher, the unquestionably brilliant American economist and statistician (arguably the first celebrity economist), who, at the height of his career, publicly proclaimed in the fall of 1929 that the stock market had reached 'a permanently high plateau'. Nine days later the devastating Wall Street crash ushered in the world's worst depression.

In 1998 NASA lost the multi-million-dollar Mars Climate Orbiter when it unexpectedly and spectacularly crashed into Mars instead of orbiting the planet to gather data, as it was supposed to do. Why? Almost unbelievably, it was because NASA's astronomical engineers had done some of the critical calculations without converting the units they were working with from imperial into metric. Remember these were experts!

Or, once again, consider the vainglorious claim of so-called experts that the *Titanic* was unsinkable. James Cameron, who directed the eponymous film of the ill-fated ship's only voyage, famously said, 'The *Titanic* is a metaphor for life ... [in a sense] we are all on the *Titanic*'.

So, believer, agnostic or atheist it is probably true to say that this book could not have been written by anyone burdened with too intellectual a mindset, governed by the strictures of a rigorous scientific, theological or academic training.

If this book had to be reduced to a two-word description, I would paraphrase and adapt from Rabbi Hillel by saying it is about love and hope – 'Love ... the rest is just commentary'.

The last lines of Philip Larkin's famous poem 'An Arundel Tomb' adds further depth, 'to prove our almost-instinct almost true:/ What will survive of us is love.'

In terms of hope, that hope ultimately needs to become grounded in faith, faith in a purpose for your life, and therefore faith in a creative force, creator or intelligent designer, that some may choose to give a name to.

Our lives – every life – has a purpose and every life matters. Cultivate a deep sense of wonder; be sure in your hope, for hope is the certainty that things will be all right in the end, no matter how they turn out. And regard the little hedgehog of doubt as your friend, because without it you cannot have faith. This is a hedgehog that, in today's cynical world, is becoming as much 'endangered' as the engaging little hedgerow creature beloved of all.

Just stop to think – really think – about how we, the whole of humanity, with every creature, plant, tree, bush and seed, all exist on this tiny little planet Earth: our 'spaceship' sailing silently alone out in the vast blackness of the infinite universe. We, each of us, have an awesome responsibility in our duty of care for each other and the only known environment in which we can live. All the more so, if this was a gift of creation with which we have been entrusted.

What I have attempted to do here is to bring together my research into diverse positions, situations and opinions, weigh them up, draw my own conclusions and present them for others to draw theirs. In the wise words of the theologian and mystic Thomas Merton, 'As human beings we are challenged to keep searching. To do anything else would be dishonest.'

I hope that in some way this little book may prove to be the starting point on what, of necessity, will be a lifelong journey of search for those still seeking meaning to their lives. Let it be an exciting journey of discovery – there is just so much to find for those who seek!

Everything will be all right in the end and, if it is not all right, it is not yet the end.

From the film *The Best Exotic Marigold Hotel*

To conclude this book even-handedly between those inclined to believe in an intelligent designer and those who are confident in their atheism, I quote from Mark Twain a statement that can be claimed as justification for their beliefs by either side:

It ain't what you don't know that gets you into trouble. It's what you know for sure that just ain't so.

Postscript

In the interest of full disclosure, in case any readers find themselves wondering about my own personal choice in this universal dilemma, I should say that the truly mind-blowing, unfathomable intricacies and complexities in the minutiae of what makes up life – microbial and physical – in its fragile, synergistic interconnectedness, is something so staggeringly enormous as to be beyond any rational cosmic, scientific explanation of its origin. It is this that has persuaded me to have chosen faith in a creator of our world and of the universe in which it sails.

Largely through upbringing and familiarity, my chosen path in the practice of my faith is Christianity. I do this while acknowledging the equal validity of other persuasions, and with the frank admission that I do not consider myself a 'good' Christian (whatever that may be) so much as one, who like Koko, is struggling to be kind and trying to do good – as opposed to being good! (This is not said with any false humility, more out of a brutally honest understanding of myself.) My oldest and closest male friend is an avowed atheist who, hands down, is the best 'Christian' I know.

As the capacity and power of the original 'Force', the 'Creator', 'Intelligent Designer' 'Prime Mover', or God by any name is so completely beyond the reasoning or imagining of even the brightest human minds, as a Christian, I find it more accessible and plausible to focus on the person of Jesus, as the tangible 'son of God', or God made man.

To those of some other faiths Jesus may be seen differently, but viewed nevertheless as the embodiment of an extraordinary, infinite, force of love sent both as a mediator and advocate to point humanity towards the existence of God.

Thus the premise behind the purpose of Jesus – his relevance and importance in connection to the evolution of our planet, the development of humanity and scientific understanding – is that, through him, God (as the intelligent designer) came to proclaim and inaugurate the 'kingdom of heaven' on earth. Others may attribute this to Mohammed, YHWH, the Guru Nanak, Krishna, other deities – or none.

The highly intelligent, militant, but always honest atheist, Christopher Hitchens, recognized, like C S Lewis, that the Jesus of the Bible left us with only three options in reaching any conclusion about him: either he is mad; he is bad; or ... he *is* God.

If God is love, and if the very essence of life is an everlasting love, then that may be how, in the end, life becomes eternal.

(I hope readers may be interested to learn about my other work, overleaf.)

OTHER WORK

Following the success of his debut novel *The Other Side of Loss* (sales of which now exceed 10,000 copies) Tom Vaughan is currently writing an Irish epic based on the most incredible true-life events from his family history.

Reviews of *The Other Side of Loss* include:

> 'Any novel that weaves a high-tension narrative out of two priests, prostitution, and a lottery ticket has to keep you turning the pages.'
>
> Gyles Brandreth

At the same time, Tom's uproarious account of the Juliana's Discotheque story related in his book *No Ordinary Experience* promises to bring all the joie de vivre, glamour and excitement of the '60s and '70s to a global screen audience backed by the timeless music of that epoch-making era.

Author Biography

Tom Vaughan published his first book, *No Ordinary Experience*, in 1986. This is a warts-and-all corporate biography chronicling the experiences of setting up and running a mobile discotheque business with his brother, Oliver. Starting with a £200 bank loan and an old van in 1966, Juliana's Discotheques grew to be the world's largest discotheque entertainment group of its time, employing over 800 people all around the world. In 1989 the company was sold to Wembley Plc for £30 million.

Following Juliana's, Tom developed business interests in the UK and the USA where he has been a part time resident of New Hampshire for over four decades. Indeed, New Hampshire serves as the backdrop to parts of his 2014 novel *The Other Side of Loss*, which has attracted a wide readership on both sides of the Atlantic. It landed its author a guest spot with Libby Purves on BBC Radio 4's *Midweek* programme, and generated sales that kept it regularly in the top five of Amazon's Metaphysical and Visionary best-seller listing throughout 2014/2015.

Hope ... and the Hedgehog stands in stark contrast to the glamour, excitement and hedonism of the international nightclub and discotheque scene of the 1970s and 1980s. In *Hope... and the Hedgehog* Tom has set out to combine his experience in business with a truly soul-searching quest for knowledge and understanding as he is drawn to explore the two fundamental questions of human existence: 'Where did we come from?' and 'Where are we going?'

Lightning Source UK Ltd.
Milton Keynes UK
UKHW021225140622
404397UK00006B/90